UNCOVERING YOUR POWER

The Guidebook to Escaping
Emotional and Physical Abuse

NICOLE BRITTNEY

JayMedia
Publishing

ISBN: 978-1-7334432-2-7 (Paperback)
ISBN: 978-1-7334432-3-4 (Epub)

Any references to historical events, real people, or real places are used fictitiously. Names, characters, and places are products of the author's imagination.

First printing edition 2020.

JayMedia Publishing
Laurel, MD 20708

www.publishing.jaymediagroup.net

Author Photo Credit: Dion Johnson, JayMedia Photography

You've seen the red flags. You've experienced the pain. Now, all that you want to do is get out.

We are casualties. We are victims. Our pain is felt by many, but our stories will no longer be silenced.

This book is for the survivors and those who desire to be freed...

TABLE OF CONTENTS

AUTHOR'S NOTE

There is an epidemic occurring in the United States that most people are too scared to address.

Domestic violence plagues every community, every race, every age, every state, and every city…….

Yet, most people consider domestic violence too sticky of a situation for them to proactively involve themselves in. Because of this, advice is few and far between for our victims. Many of their stories and experiences are silenced. Their needs are buried until they actively work to find resources to break through it. It takes so much strength for a woman under these circumstances to make it to the finish line.

My goal is to change that.

I have suffered from abuse. There were moments in my journey where I thought I might lose my mind. I was scared for myself, confused about my future, and overwhelmed beyond reason about my current situation and what I needed to do to change it. I remember praying for a savior and wishing there was some guidebook to help me break free! But no such savior ever came. I had to work through the process and educate myself. It took me over a year to find freedom. I pray that no other woman feels as isolated and alone as I did during that time of my life.

If you are looking for relief, I hope this book provides you with a stepping stone to freeing yourself. If no one ever told you, you deserve the best of the best in relationships. That starts with a healthy partner and a healthy foundation.

If you are trying to uncover whether or not you're in an abusive relationship, this book is for you. If you're looking for a way out of your abusive relationship, this book is for you. If you're trying to support a friend or family member suffering from abuse, this book is for you. Lastly, if you're looking to understand a person who you think may be abusing another, this book is for you.

It takes a community to support one another. The worst thing that you can do is turn a blind eye to abuse. Whether you are the victim, a friend or relative of the victim, or even the abuser, we all have a part in bettering our communities and freeing ourselves from mental and physical bondage.

No matter your role, you can be a part of the solution if you choose to.

With love,

Nicole

Chapter 1

A HISTORY OF ABUSE

I remember the first time my relationship got physical.

I remember every moment and every thought that followed. I will for the rest of my life.

My abuser was always right by my side to both hurt and comfort me, all in the same breath. He became my pain and my healer and in offering himself as such, I was drawn in on a deeper level.

I needed him. It felt that way at least. He possessed a familiar type of love.

Yes, he was my abuser and I knew that I should run, but he was also my comfort. He was my only friend at the time and the only one who knew our dirty little secret: that I had let a man hit me and stayed with him anyway.

I didn't share my experiences with anyone at the beginning. For at least a year, I kept it all to myself. There was one occasion, within that first year, where my mate's best friend and brother witnessed his outrage towards me and held him back, but otherwise, every encounter was private and a 'me versus him' experience.

Manipulation would follow with my partner's most sincere apologies and acts of kindness. His explaining to me how I was at fault and how if I would just be a better woman, in some manner or fashion, the instance would never occur again. Typically, the conversation didn't even go that far. We simply wouldn't discuss it and would act as if it never occurred or only discuss it once and then never again. If I tried to bring it up, I was 'stuck in the past' and not focused on growth and that was enough for me to let it go. After all, I wanted to be a part of the solution, not the problem.

This absence of addressing the issue and resolving it left me feeling very empty and confused. It was as if my experience was all in my mind and not as big of a deal as it felt in my heart. I'd urge for change to ears not equipped to listen and that cycle became the foundation upon which our relationship was built. Yes, my partner loved me, but he could not control his rage and I held onto hope that with time and effort, he would change.

People who have never experienced abuse may be confused by this description.

There is a notion that a well put together, successful woman, could not possibly settle for such a mate. Therefore, if that is her experience, she must be flawed. Something must be wrong with her.

Perhaps.

But every black woman is searching for a love that most of us have never experienced, which makes us vulnerable to all kinds of attacks in the name of love.

Even aside from being black and coming from our shared experiences, *any* woman and *any* man could quite *possibly* find themselves victim to manipulation, control, or abuse of some form in their lifetime.

This is *especially* true amongst people of color in America.

I know this because I've lived this. And this is a book of my experiences.

If you'd like the insight from someone with credentials whose never actually lived a day in our communities and can't truly understand what it's like to grow up in a black family or be involved in a black relationship, have at it. There are plenty of resources to choose from.

I choose to share my story in a way that my community can connect with. I don't want to preach to you or offer you some list of statistics. This book is about real life, from a real woman who's lived it.

I know my community because I am a part of it and I'd like to share my experience in hopes that it helps you to navigate through yours. A look at the factors that have contributed to some of the harm within our relationships will help us to understand how to resolve it.

With that in mind, let's address how history has set the stage for a line of division between the black man and the black woman.

Chapter 2

THE PAST AFFECTS YOUR FUTURE

We first learn about relationships and the characteristics of a healthy relationship from our families. If we witness abuse, neglect, or mistreatment within our household, we *typically* either internalize or repel that energy. So as adults, we become the similar person or complete opposite of what we've seen as children.

Sadly, both sets of traits could quite possibly be toxic to our future relationships.

Let's discuss the typical backgrounds that we find in the experiences of many of my peers, the 80's babies of America.

First, you have the children who grew up in households with both a healthy mother and a healthy father. Children that grew up in a healthy family environment likely grew up to understand a man's role in his family and how he expresses love to his wife and children. This child will also gain an understanding of a woman's role in the household and how she might nurture and express love to her husband and children. This child was raised with an example of a family unit and the individual traits of both a healthy man and a healthy woman.

Hopefully, taking on familial roles, establishing confidence within themselves as an adult, and later searching for a mate is an easier process because of the environment that *this* child was raised in. No matter how weird, silly, strict or even out of touch this person's parents were, they still offered their child an example of what a healthy family unit consisted of and how a husband and wife might interact and raise their children within that unit.

This child was given a foundation upon which to grow. Their growth as an adult will be up to the decisions they make with the values and expectations that were instilled in them at a young age.

This individual's parents would be considered the GOAT's of our generation! With all the odds against them, they still managed to raise their family as a familial unit and in doing so, their children will not have to break the generational curse that many of us will break during our time here on earth.

Next in line is the child who had both parents but witnessed one of their parents, or both, being talked down to or abused in some form or fashion.

Abuse and manipulation come in a number of forms and could include verbal abuse, physical abuse, belittling, instilling fear, or manipulating a person's mind so that they might act in a specific manner or under a specific form of control.

This child may grow to embrace traits of one or even both of their parents. They could embrace traits of both the abuser and the victim or they could lean heavily in one direction or the other. This child will step into life as an adult with a very confused idea of what love and a healthy relationship really is. They may have to detox themselves mentally from the abuse they witnessed as a child to make room for new values that promote a healthy individual and familial approach to their life.

Next up is the amazingly large number of African American children who were raised without any sort of father figure in the home what-so-ever. These children may have never witnessed their mother in a long term, healthy relationship with *anyone*.

This has become another very confusing foundation where a child might develop and define their understanding of a healthy family unit from television, a peer, a mentor, religion or some other outside source. With no guidance in how to find a proper example, and so many media outlets selling dreams of the "perfect family", a number of challenges can come from this sort of self-teaching. Children of this background may find themselves out of touch with reality and what a healthy relationship really consists of as an adult.

Then, there are those of us who were passed through the system – foster care, adoption, group homes. If you grew up in a group home, for example, you will have had *no* exposure to a healthy family unit and you may grow up without ever having anyone who was 'just for you' and nurtured you as such. This person may not only struggle with relationships but even love for themselves could be difficult to find as an adult.

All of these scenarios *negate* the growth and nurturing a child needs to grow up healthy, strong, and confident in themselves, yet all of these scenarios are familiar if not the life of most of my generation. These *scenarios* are a part of us and have stripped the black community down to the bare bones and confusion that you see today.

This is by design.

The black man and woman have been victim to attacks on the black family from the time we were kidnapped from our countries up to today.

These attacks led to the challenges highlighted above and that only names a few. The black family in America is as complicated as it gets, and we hold a number of backgrounds and experiences that many other races could not imagine.

Today, it is difficult for us as a community to even begin

to comprehend that. Many of our ancestors' stories have been silenced. Yet, bits of the truth are still available to those who seek it. Whether you choose to study our past or not, the living proof of its impact is apparent today, in 2019, in our families, within our individual walks of life, and most certainly, in our romantic relationships.

We have to address and understand our past in order to be freed from the bondage it has captured us in. That bondage is our current state of being, and we have to rise above it to progress successfully as a people in this country.

This starts with a focus on the black community and improving our relationships or leaving them for those that better serve our needs. This action will offer a stepping stone to laying the foundation necessary for us to break from generational bondage.

Please understand, this attack on the black family did not come without reason. It was tactical in its approach and this country has funneled billions, upon billions, *upon billions* of dollars and years of resources into breaking the black family down, *strategically*.

So, before you beat yourself up about your current state of relations, understand that you are not alone and this is something many of your brothers and sisters are working to overcome as well.

The black man has always been positioned to be a threat of some kind. For generations, this has been the case. We, as a people, have internalized the same ideas that this country has used to push their agenda and scare society from the 'threat of the black man' or the inappropriate 'sexual nature' of the black woman.

Black women have internalized a fear and resentment of the black man. Black men have internalized a total disregard and lack of respect for the black woman. Black men and women have internalized and taken on negative traits that we describe as 'the culture' in order to escape feelings of inferiority. Instead, we as a people embrace the stereotypical traits and flaunt them so that we can feel like we are a part of this society without shame.

In the large scheme of things, the war against us seems to be a success. We have become the very monsters they have illustrated us to be. All of this has been a breeding ground for confusion, insecurity, anger, resentment, hate and harm within our communities and families.

All of which, we take out on each other.

It's no wonder that we are in the state we are in - we were targeted, and this was a part of the plan. It's been affecting our families for hundreds of years in this country but because of advances in technology and access to educational resources, now is the time that we can fight back in an effort to return structure to our communities and family units.

It starts by turning away from abuse, manipulation, and control tactics within our romantic relationships. We must heal and encourage those in need of healing to seek it. That means turning away from what is toxic and what does not lay a foundation for the families we need in our community.

In doing so, those that need help will be forced to seek it. We are not looking to isolate or divide but instead to encourage growth within our brothers and sisters that need it.

The cycle stops with you.

When you break down a cycle as powerful and as deeply rooted as this, you will realize the truth…

That you my dear, can move mountains with just the thought.

Chapter 3

THE HONEYMOON PHASE

When a woman meets a new man, the sky's the limit, as far as her imagination goes! It's a beautiful feeling meeting someone you can connect with and knowing that they feel the connection too. It's heaven and one of the best feelings for both men and women. Because finding that connection comes so few and far between, it's natural to want to embrace it….

Dwayne and Michelle had only been dating for a couple of weeks but Michelle could tell that Dwayne was ready to make a commitment. He had already taken her out on three dates and he texted her sweet nothings every night and every morning.

Michelle was falling, and she was falling quickly!

She kept telling herself, "Slow it down! You've only known him a couple of weeks!"

But it felt so good chatting with Dwayne, and he had already shared with Michelle that he thought she was 'the one'. Slow down for what?! Michelle was enjoying the moment and wanted to take it to the next level with Dwayne.

On the Tuesday of their third week of dating, Dwayne asked Michelle out for coffee. When she met him at the coffee shop, he met her with a rose and a smile.

"You look beautiful, Michelle!" Dwayne shared.

Michelle was smiling from ear to ear and just needed to reapply her lip gloss so the smiling and chatting could continue! They grabbed coffee and stepped outside to catch up. Dwayne started the conversation with a request. He wanted Michelle to consider being his girlfriend.

While Michelle was caught off guard, she was flattered that Dwayne chose her!

"How did you know I was the one so quickly," she asked.

"When you know, you just know baby," Dwayne responded. They sipped their coffee, chatted for a bit and began to officially date.

In Michelle's eyes, nothing could go wrong!

Michelle and Dwayne's relationship started out on a great foot. It moved quickly, but it felt good to both Dwayne and Michelle. Without context into their dating conversations, it's hard to tell if they jumped in too quickly, or not. It's also a matter of personal opinion…

Manipulators love the Honeymoon Phase too! While we shouldn't go into any new relationship with preconceived notions, the Honeymoon Phase should be sought after with some level of reason. After all, this is a new relationship and someone you will grow to learn. The only way that you can learn about another person is with time. It's important that you not slip into dating with an emotional lens. A careful woman will want to be observant during this stage so that she can really understand her new, potential mate.

There are some key areas you want to observe and be aware of before investing in a new, long term relationship.

UNDERSTAND YOUR NEW MATES LIVING AND FINANCIAL SITUATIONS

Before dating, you should understand what you'd like out of a new relationship. Are you interested in dating just to date? Are you looking for a lifetime commitment or marriage? You want to understand your basic needs before falling head over heels for someone who may or may not be a fit.

Once you've uncovered your basic needs, you should approach dating in a fashion that uncovers whether or not your potential new mate meets those criteria. If you are looking for a long-term commitment but your potential mate could never see themselves staying with a woman for more than a couple of years, that may not be a fit! Asking open ended questions and understanding your date's past relationships can help you gain insight into where they stand in their level of commitment.

If you are looking for a long-term commitment, or even if you are not, you will want to learn as much as you can about your mate's living and financial situation. It's important to tread carefully here. You don't want to seem like you're only interested in financial gain! But, if you all are to co-exist, even for a short time, it's important to be honest and understand the truth of your potential partner's situation.

I know these new Instagram memes are all the rave but a few hold true. A-many-a homeless men have gotten their come up and new place from dating and moving in with an unknowing woman too quickly. Sis, don't let this be you! Understand whether or not your new mate can afford to support himself, even if it's with roommates. Know whether or not your new mate lives with their parents. Even if it's temporary, it's valuable information! Know whether or not your new mate lives with an ex-girlfriend or child's mother. This could come up in the future and it's better for you to know what you're getting yourself into early in the game!

Understanding your potential new mate's financial situation could take time, and I don't encourage a lot of prying here. A man will *show* you what you need to see with time. Small actions can help to highlight whether or not he is willing to act as a provider, an equal, or a leech. Let's be honest, each subset of men has their choice of women who are willing to accept them just as they are! Keep in mind that men often times have a harder time finding success than we have as black women. On the other hand, there is a large community of professional black men that would knock your socks off with their levels of success and knowledge in their fields. Point being - you have choices. You don't have to settle.

You need to understand your needs to find a mate that meets them. Make sure you're making a commitment to someone that you can love just as they are because that's all that's promised. The worst thing that you can do as a woman is to accept a man for who he is, only to diss him for it a few short months later. Be fair with yourself and be fair with him.

Ask open ended questions. Observe. Ask to visit. Ask for another date. Ask to meet his friends. Ask to meet his parents. Do what you can to uncover what you can because that's the only way you'll learn the truth. If something seems off, address it and pay attention to the responses you receive. If you see a red flag, take two steps back and plan time to observe more.

It's not that you need to know everything, but it's up to you to uncover game and act accordingly. Trust me, your potential new mate may not be forthcoming, but if they are willing to take their time, you will learn all you need to know in the process.

If they are not willing to take their time, start firing off those questions and listen! Please keep in mind, he has a choice to tell you a lie or the truth. But with limited time to observe, you won't know what's what either way... I encourage you to tread lightly! What you can't get out of conversation, make sure you're setting aside a mental note to observe.

Chapter 4

OH, I THINK I LIKE HIM...

About a month into the relationship, Michelle was all kinds of in love with her new man, Dwayne!

Dwayne was handsome, fit, dark, and those eyes!!! She couldn't get enough.

Michelle and Dwayne were seeing each other four to five times a week. On the days Michelle didn't want to get together, she did so anyway just to show Dwayne how interested and available she was to him.

She wanted him to see that he was right to choose her and that she would work to keep him.

Dwayne was soaking it all in with regular visits to Michelle's place. She could cook some bangin' ass ribs and the

19

image of her whipping it up was even better. Michelle had curves in all the right places. Got damn! He couldn't wait to dive into that.

He decided one night during a visit that he'd try his chance at spending the night. He'd been taking Michelle out for over a month and had all kinds of ideas for things they could do with the right time and the right lighting.

He licked his lips as Michelle finished setting up the table and preparing his meal.

"Stop baby, I'm finishing up this mac-and-cheese. Boy, you gon' make me burn something!"

Michelle laughed as Dwayne brushed up against her firmly. His arms wrapped around her waist as he moved in close, cornering her at the stove. From the back he whispered sweet nothings into her ear. Pushing up harder ...Michelle pushed back.

"Chill, it's getting hot in here," she pleaded with a slight moan.

"The only thing that's gonna chill is you," Dwayne replied licking his lips and moving her towards the sectional. "Get over here, girl."

Michelle couldn't resist. Four weeks in and enough was enough. She wanted to take her time, but she wanted Dwayne more. And she would gladly have him tonight.

They kissed. And they did their thing.

ARE THEY SLEEPING WITH ANYONE ELSE?

We live in a time where people are very open to sleeping around and having multiple sexual partners. You will want to uncover, before lying down with this person, what their current sexual lifestyle is.

I won't get too in the nitty gritty on this one. Everyone has their own idea of sexual pleasure, when to give it, what it entails, etc.

I encourage sisters to get to know their mate and establish boundaries for how quickly they become sexual. Once you become sexual with a man, reason goes out the window and you are in that moment, and to follow, emotionally connected to him. You have limited your ability to view him through a lens of reason. He has now seen your most intimate self. He has nothing else to desire or imagine because you've shown him all of you.

Whether you like it or not, that gives him the upper hand in the relationship and he no longer has anything that he has to work for. The conquest is over and you my dear have been won! And, if he's sleeping with another woman and you're not aware, he will likely continue to. After all, now he has the both of you. So what you didn't know?! As far as he's concerned, you didn't ask. You allowed it.

Men think differently than women and it's important to assess where he is mentally, and in this case, sexually. It will tell you a lot about your new mate. But once you lay down with him, you can consider your vision just a bit more blurred than it was prior to the sexual connection.

Remove the flesh. Remove any sources of energy that limit your ability to act with reason as you pursue your new guy. Understand his sexual background before you lay down with him. Your health, your womb, your body, and your future all depend on each and every decision that *you* make. Especially those that involve heavy connections coming into your life.

Your body is your temple. Your womb is sacred ground.

Know who you are dealing with before you take it there. Time reveals all.

Chapter 5

THE RED FLAG

I remember hearing once…that love is free. Love is the freedom to be who you are and to be loved for it. To walk in your journey, your way, and to have a companion that allows you the space to do so comfortably.

I've never experienced a love like that.

I have always considered myself a traditional woman. I have believed and still believe in gender roles. I *believed* in submitting to a man. I thought it made me a better woman. I thought it set me apart. What I didn't know is just how far this idea of submission could go when presented to the wrong environment and relationship.

Submission became so much more than I expected it to be.

Submission became cooking and cleaning and caring for the home with no help. Submission became caring for my mate's child without his assistance or consistent presence. Submission became financially providing for my family during hard times that turned into consistent times. Submission became forgiving him for infidelity. Submission became keeping my mouth shut when I was spoken down to, even if it was in the most demeaning fashion. Submission became keeping secrets behind closed doors that I was not able to speak of or even acknowledge.

Submission became an expectation, and then submission became a way of life.

It became the chains that kept me bound to depression, unhappiness, and abuse.

Submission took away my worth, my value, and the expectation to be shown that I was valued by my partner. I gave this idea of submission to the wrong relationships, the wrong people, and the wrong environments.

I still very highly believe in the importance of gender roles and identification. I even still believe that being a submissive woman is helpful to balancing a relationship. You just have to ensure that you're giving it to the right person.

Because the black family has been under attack for so many generations, our ability to cohabitate and trust each other in a healthy way has been shattered.

It is so important that our men work to heal and acknowledge their role in the black family. It is also important that we as women heal and work to identify our role, our power, our presence and our value in the black family as well.

When both genders understand and accept their role in building and bettering the black relationship, we will find a more harmonious union where we can work together to lay the foundation we so desperately need.

DO THEY HAVE CHILDREN?

You're probably thinking, hey - what does all of this have to do with power, abuse, and manipulation anyway? Trust me, uncovering potential strains to your relationship early will help you to join in union with an understanding and acceptance of one another. It will also allow you to uncover what may or may not work for you so that you can move accordingly.

So, this one's simple. Does he have children? How many children does he have? Does he claim his children? Does he talk about his children? Does he father his children? How does he raise his children? How interactive is he within their lives? What's his relationship with his child(ren's) mother?

All of these are questions you will want to be aware of before moving forward. If you build a long-term relationship with this man, his children will also affect your life.

Make sure that the both of you are on the same page.

If he doesn't have children, it may be a good idea for you to ask open ended questions about his plans on building a family. This is valuable insight and a window into his soul and whether or not he wants to build a legacy, or just live life! With all types of different interests and backgrounds, you would be silly not to have this sort of discussion before lying down, before meeting family, and before committing to this new, potential boo.

Chapter 6

THE FIGHT FOR RESPECT

Michelle was frustrated. She and Dwayne had been dating for four months now and intimate for the last three. But lately, Dwayne was distant and even cold at times. The sex was AMAZING. Dwayne was dominant and strong and would have his way with Michelle, and she loved his sexual confidence and assertiveness. She was happy to be the woman of his world; however, Michelle found that he was not as engaged in the conversation as he used to be and they tended to do whatever Dwayne wanted with little regard for what Michelle might have had going on or wanted to do.

Michelle considered it a result of Dwayne's dominant personality. He knew what he wanted out of life and had chosen Michelle to walk hand in hand with him as he fulfilled it. She wouldn't complain. It's not often that you find a black man willing to commit and she was not about to just give that away.

She would fight for her King.

And she did.

Three months in, Michelle found out that Dwayne still had a relationship with an ex that he still deeply cared for. He wasn't ready to let it go and it was putting a strain on Dwayne and Michelle's new relationship.

Michelle had given him the green light to return to his ex once she was aware of the circumstances. Oh, you thought you could have us both?! Nah my brother, you have to make a choice.

And Dwayne chose Michelle.

But something was still just off.

Dwayne was spending more and more time on his phone. He was moody, often. He had even begun speaking recklessly to Michelle. He wasn't calling her out of her name or throwing insults, but instead his tone with Michelle changed. It was more demanding. Less comforting. And this air of tension was present more and more often as they spent time together.

Dwayne barely ever asked how Michelle was anymore, and he was irritated by all the questions she'd bring to the table about his ex. She tried to let it go. But midnight texts and hushed phone calls made it hard for Michelle to remain confident in herself.

"What does this chick have that I don't", she thought. "I'll *show Dwayne. I'm the best thing he will ever have."*

There were times Michelle wondered if she was continuing to invest in Dwayne because of their connection or because of the competition brewing between Michelle and Dwayne's ex. Either way, Michelle had no intention of bowing down to either stressor. She was a strong, black, educated, and beautiful woman. What more could Dwayne want?!

As far as Michelle was concerned, he needed her.

ACTIONS SPEAK LOUDER THAN WORDS

So cliché! But the truth behind this saying stands true. You cannot truly learn a person without seeing their actions and reactions to different situations. It's important that you take the time to really observe your new mate.

In the early stages of dating, it's as simple as observing how they speak to and treat others. A restaurant location is a great place to gain an understanding of how this person starts a conversation, interacts with wait staff, and carries themselves in public. Are they making eye contact when they talk to you? Are they asking you questions to really get to know you? Is the conversation all about them? Are they trying to sell themselves? Are they rude to the wait staff? Did they tip?

There is so much you can gain from very simple interactions. You can't get too caught up on a whim that you're not taking in your surroundings and observing your date's traits during this time. Make sure that what you're observing aligns with your personality, goals, and moral character. If you are not aware of these things, it's important that you take a step back from dating until you take the time to truly learn yourself.

Whether we care to acknowledge it or not, nine times out of ten, our abusers show their true colors early on in the relationship. We can choose to ignore signs of dysfunction, we can choose to forgive disrespect, or we can choose to work through infidelity, but we need to understand that every choice we make has an outcome and plays a role in the future of that relationship.

When you aim to show the world why you should be respected, you realize that the act of even trying to prove your worth falls on deaf ears.

If you have to fight for respect, it was never there to begin with.

Stop trying to get respect from people who don't have it within themselves to give.

We have to stop thinking that a seed not properly nourished will bloom. It can. And it will. *If* it aims to and if it seeks the nourishment needed to develop. But its cycle of growth is going to look a little different than the seed who received proper sunshine, water, affection, and love.

Some of us have been so damaged during our walk in life that we don't have a fountain of love, affection, and nourishment within us to give the world. Please understand, before you can give these gifts to the world, you have to give them to yourself.

Most of us grew up in backgrounds that did not properly nurture growth. Black men and women don't have the familial foundation that other cultures in America have. *We are building it right now as we speak!* And many of us are struggling to do so because we don't know what the end result looks like - we've never seen it before. But, it is our responsibility to our culture and to our children to lay a better foundation than what was afforded to us.

Before you beg for respect from someone who has shown they don't have it for you, ask yourself, '*why*'? Why do you desire their respect? Do you understand what respect, love and consideration for mankind really is? If so, why do you have to beg for it? If you do, something is not balanced in the relationship you seek respect from.

Your next action is to identify what that imbalance may be and work to resolve it or walk away.

That decision alone will be what impacts your fate, and I'm sorry but there is no right answer. There is only what you know and desire of your life and what you accept. Please understand that when the two don't align, it *will* have an effect on your relationship.

We can no longer ignore blazing red flags in the hopes that they will just begin to lessen with time. We have to acknowledge them. We have to understand them. We have to work together to resolve them. Or, we have to move on and allow for more growth within ourselves and look for the source of the red flag(s) in question.

This is going to be imperative to healing individually and then healing the black family as a whole. We can't keep pushing our problems under a rug and then lifting that rug in a few days with the expectation that the dirt will be gone. The dirt is there and now it's mixed with dust, darkness, and even more mess. The more we cover it up, the nastier and stinkier it is up under our rug.

We have to do better. We have to start breaking down these challenges for what they really are and attacking them. We can no longer accept the mess or it will follow us and stink up everything we have worked to build.

Chapter 7

THE FIRST TIME...

Most of the time, we don't identify the true red flags until the relationship has turned the corner of no return. More often than not, we're discussing the identified red flags in hindsight to something major taking place. Then, the conversations with our families and friends reveal the truth that we were too lost in the moment to see.....

Michelle and Dwayne had seen a difficult past couple of weeks, so Michelle smiled from ear to ear when Dwayne mentioned his plans to take her out to dinner and a movie later that night.

Michelle had really been considering the value of her

relationship with Dwayne and where it was headed. With the bad air of tension they'd met recently, Michelle wondered if Dwayne might need some time to get things in order on his end. He'd never admitted to still dating his ex, but the signs were there and Michelle thought, "Maybe a step back would be good for us."

But just as the thought crossed her mind, the text invitation hit the lock screen and she just knew it was meant to be. "Dinner and a movie it is," She smirked to herself.

"I'm about to get cute and show this man just what he's getting when it comes to me", she thought playfully.

Two hours, a beat face and sexy dress later, Michelle anxiously awaited Dwayne's call that he was on the way to pick her up.

Instead, she saw the Chrysler 300 whip around the corner to her neighborhood. She was out the door in 2 seconds flat and damn near sitting on Dwayne's lap in 3. They embraced one another and made a move.

Dinner was perfect. They had a nice chill meal at a Tex-Mex restaurant and then went to the bar next door for drinks before the movie. Dwayne seemed relaxed and cool. He didn't talk much but his charm was appealing and his smile contagious, so Michelle took the opportunity to talk about herself and the crazy work week she'd experienced. In the midst of moving into her family update, she took a hard look at Dwayne who was gazing at something a little too hard for her liking.

"Dwayne, baby, you listening to me?" she asked.

He nodded, tilted down his shades, and shifted his attention back to his date.

That instance quickly left Michelle's mind, her one-sided conversation continued and soon enough, they were off to the movie. Michelle was happy to share Dwayne's company and she wasn't about to be one of those nagging chicks that had an issue with every little thing.

Dwayne bought Michelle a dozen roses on the way to the movie which helped to calm any reservations she previously had about their relationship. They enjoyed an amazing night together that ended with Dwayne on top of Michelle.

Yeah. Their connection was like that…

So the next morning, when Michelle woke up to an empty bed, she was confused.

The next morning turned into the next day. The next day into the next week…and suddenly five days had passed with no text, no phone call, and certainly no visit from Dwayne.

Michelle called Dwayne until her call log was filled with calls and her eyes filled with tears.

"Fuck. How could I be so stupid?!" she couldn't help but ask herself.

"That's it, if he calls - I'm laying him out and moving on!" she promised herself. No tears were even worth what he could have controlled with the proper communication.

But the fact that he left the door wide open with no explanation kept Michelle cycling the events of their relationship over and over in her head. "Did I do something wrong? Maybe say something I shouldn't have? Was I too into myself at the bar last weekend? What happened?", she pondered over and over and over and over again in her mind.

Until the phone rang.

Her heart raced.

"Hello?"

"How's my princess?"

Michelle. Went. Crazy.

"Dwayne, how dare you not call me for a week and hey princess me now! Where are you?!"

"I'm sitting outside your place," he responded.

Michelle almost jumped from her seat with joy. She ran to the bathroom. Sprayed on some good scents, tidied up a bit, and ran to greet her boo.

"But I can't be too easy on him," she thought, as she worked her way down the stairs to open the door.

"We gotta talk," Michelle urged.

"Nah. We gotta catch up." Dwayne flirted, un-tied Michelle's robe, and caught up the best way he knew how, in the bedroom.

An hour passed in what felt like a few moments and they relaxed in Michelle's bed comforted by their sexual encounter.

Michelle waited as long as she could before working up the nerve to address the elephant in the room.

"Dwayne, what happened? Why didn't you call me all week?" she asked.

"Look, work was stressing me and I just needed a little time to myself." he claimed.

Michelle thought about her next question before firing

off too quickly. After all, she didn't want to chase him away. At the same time she wanted to set some boundaries and let Dwayne know that she wasn't just any ol' type of woman and what a commitment truly meant to her.

So she was quiet when the next question rolled off her tongue, "were you with her?"......

"Man. Fuck outta here with that shit, Michelle! I can't even visit for a few minutes without you starting with the bull! Look, I gotta get out of here."

Dwayne headed to the bathroom before Michelle could get her next word out, leaving her standing in the empty bedroom, speechless.

Dwayne's phone sat on the dresser where he had placed it before undressing. Michelle took a split second to check the home screen.

Incoming Text:
Ashley 757 - Hey handsome. We still meeting up tonight?

Michelle tried every code under the sun that she could think of before Dwayne re-entered the bedroom.

"What you doin' chelle? Oh, that's how we going now. You just going to go through my stuff like that?!" Michelle could sense the energy but didn't want to give up that easy.

"Whose Ashley 757, Dwayne?"

"Is she why you've been MIA on me all week?"

"Fuck outta here, Michelle, I don't know what you talkin' about."

"Well I got her number and best believe I'll ask her myself right……."

SLAP.

Before Michelle could get the sentence out, Dwayne had slapped stars to the side of her left eye.

She fell to the floor, totally speechless.

No man had ever laid a hand on Michelle. She choked back tears while Dwayne gathered himself and seemed to realize what he'd just done.

"See?! This why you can't be all up in my face with this crazy shit, woman," he explained.

Dwayne leaned over to help Michelle up.

"Look baby, I'm sorry," he said immediately. "I don't know what got into me. I told you I've been stressed lately. I need you to be my princess. The last thing I need is for you to add to the crazy in my life. I need you to be my peace," he claimed.

"Fuck."

"I hate that I just did that."

Michelle sat on the bed, still speechless for what seemed like forever.

She didn't know what to say. She didn't know what to do. She knew what she just experienced had crossed an unacceptable line. But she was too stuck in the moment to address it.

"Look, Ima get out of your hair, Michelle."

Dwayne stood up, gathered his belongings, and dipped.

Michelle cried tears that she had never cried before that day. Dwayne had tarnished a piece of her womanhood that she would never quite recover from.

She sat in darkness with thoughts that she might drown in her own bed of tears that night.

Chapter 8

CYCLES OF ABUSE

⁓∽◦∾◦⁓

Michelle was exhausted.

She'd been dating Dwayne for a year and two months now and while she'd seen a lot of improvement in Dwayne's efforts within their relationship, they still struggled with stability and disrespect aimed at one another.

Michelle thought back to the first time Dwayne had gotten physical in her home...

Later, after the occurrence, she found a dozen roses at her doorstep one random morning.

She'd received several letters on her car and in her mailbox to follow. They were sweet nothings urging Michelle to call Dwayne so they could talk. It took her two weeks to do so, but eventually she called and Michelle and Dwayne chose to set aside their differences and continue building their relationship.

Dwayne argued that with all the struggles he'd seen in life, a good woman could help him soften his aggression and be more dedicated to growth in his life and career. He wanted to be a man of God, and he asked Michelle to stand with him.

It all sounded so good and it was all Michelle ever wanted out of life. She loved that he wanted her as badly as she wanted him. She could be patient for the cause and she felt in her heart the end result would be the love and family she had yearned for her whole life.

Dwayne was the one.

The couple enjoyed the fall season together that year on into the holidays. Everything seemed to flow well until Christmas came and Dwayne began his disappearing act again.

It hurt Michelle to the core.

She would wait up, nights for him with no call, no text, no update or even apology upon his return. Dwayne ran the game and Michelle was submissive to his needs. She wanted to just be a lady and show him that she could help calm his high energy and restless spirit.

Michelle wanted to be the one to save Dwayne.

She didn't look at it exactly that way, but her efforts reflected that goal.

During their first Christmas together, Dwayne set expectations that he was a family man and would spend that time with his family. He'd check in with Michelle mid-way during the day so they could meet up and exchange gifts, but he'd otherwise be unavailable. Michelle was understanding since the expectation was set but when Christmas day came, she didn't hear from Dwayne or take part in the visit they planned because she was unable to reach Dwayne for the entirety of the day.

Sadly, Michelle didn't have family in the area and had stayed in town just to see her man.

She was completely devastated when their plans fell through and she drove four hours home to her family that night to get away.

When Michelle returned to the area, she still hadn't heard from Dwayne and felt like enough was enough, she would track him down and break up with him and move on with her life.

Michelle visited Dwayne's local gym, best friend's home, his work place, and church. It seemed like he was dodging her but she was going to have her final word and be respected. She stopped by a local bar he visited frequently and found him there enjoying a drink at the bar, alone.

"Thank God," she thought before approaching.

Before Michelle could get the words she had planned all out, Dwayne spotted her and turned on his charm.

"Michelle baby! Don't be sneaking up on me like that wit yo fineeee self…."

From the smell of his breath, he had been drinking way too much for her liking.

"Dwayne… let me take you home."

Michelle felt his safety was the biggest concern upon seeing his current state and opted to take him to her place where they could chat after he sobered up.

When the couple got home it seemed Dwayne had a burst of energy that he didn't have at the bar or drive home. He wanted Michelle but Michelle did not plan to give in. A lot of their arguments had just been ironed over with sex, and she was tired of the cycle. He would sober up and they would address their problems together.

Dwayne didn't want to sober up that night.

He became increasingly irritated and impatient with Michelle's choice to not satisfy his sexual needs.

"Oh, so you think you all that, huh?" Dwayne challenged Michelle.

"Dwayne, I just think it's best you relax here in the living room and I'll go to my room. We ain't even gotta take it there tonight."

"You ain't runnin' shit!"

"Dwayne, baby, I'm not trying to run shit." Michelle's voice trailed as she tried to leave the room.

"Come back here!"

"Dwayne, what?! I can't do this tonight!!"

"That's what's wrong with you black women. Don't never want to listen. Always thinking you the shit. Get yo ass over here! YOU came looking for me! You will respect me!"

Michelle was not about to tolerate Dwayne's shit that night after all that she had been through over the holidays and in trying to find him.

"Look, Dwayne. I'm a good woman but don't push me."

"I'll do what the fuck I want," he challenged.

Dwayne got up and stood toe to toe with Michelle as if she was his homie taking shit.

He put his fingers to her face and spit in it.

"Don't ever fucking disrespect me. And don't you ever go looking for me unless I want to fucking be found."

He grabbed Michelle by the throat and held her there. She submitted to his force and they spent the rest of that evening in silence.

This was the second physical altercation the couple had.

The third came three months later and the fourth a season or so after that.

With so much time in between each occurrence, it really didn't feel like abuse to Michelle. She knew her man was aggressive and sometimes he just couldn't control his outbursts. Michelle learned how to avoid triggering the anger but she found that sooner or later, even with her best behavior, she'd find herself in a bed of tears at least every few months or so. It wasn't until the year and two month mark that she began to connect the consistency of each attack. This realization, as awakening as it was to be realistic, only made her feel worse about herself and what she had chosen to accept within her life.

This time marked a transition in Michelle. She began to not only accept Dwayne's abuse, but she began inflicting abuse towards herself as well. Michelle was caught in the cycle *and drowning in it. All she could consider was her life with Dwayne and all the mistakes she had made to get them to this point.*

Michelle had failed in the only part of her life she wanted to succeed in the most, her family.....

You will lose yourself trying to heal someone else.

YOU WILL LOSE YOURSELF TRYING TO HEAL SOMEONE ELSE

My sisters. We have got to restore our spirits, and we can't do so if we are trying to save everyone else before we get that peace within our own lives.

It's easy to find yourself lost in a person that has not truly found themselves and has anger and resentment within themselves.

We need to assess whether or not we are in a state of pain and seek healing if we are. We need to really be honest with ourselves, our experiences, and how we impact the lives of others. If you find yourself constantly speaking negatively to or about others, you may be harming the people close to you with your outlook.

We must cleanse ourselves.

Then, we must protect ourselves because the negative energy circulating in our space *does* have an effect. It *does* steal joy. Even the strongest of leaders will fall weakened by constant engagement with negative energy.

I'd like to take a few moments to share how easy it was for me, personally, to fall into a painful cycle of abuse.

Similar to Michelle, the abuse in my situation, did not occur daily. It more so deepened with each season that I accepted it. Some months we might have two to three physical encounters, while other seasons of the year we could go months with no occurrence at all.

During the peaceful times, I always had hope that we'd never experience the darkness again, but sooner or later, it would always return as quickly as it had left, and we would have to deal with the consequences in the moment and the long-term effects that it had on our relationship down the line.

At the beginning of the relationship, it looked nothing like what it looked like at the end. The abuse was masked. Physical abuse wasn't hitting, kicking, biting, etc. It was pinning me against the wall or deep holds to my wrists or upper arms. While I was taken aback by the force, my partner had not hit me and it honestly didn't occur to me that that force could one day escalate.

The verbal abuse of my experience, however, was constant.

I still remember my first date with my abuser. We both shared painful experiences from our previous relationships and I remember a comment he made to me that I should blame myself for my mistreatment because I had let a player play me again. He claimed that I should have known that's what a man would do.

I remember being taken aback at first because I was in the midst of hurting when I shared my story, but when I thought about it that evening, I appreciated his honest approach and took the time to look at how I might have harmed myself in the past.

For me, that didn't have to serve as a red flag, but because of the verbal insults that I would hear often to follow, that was the first indicator I ever saw of my ex's true mentality and thought process. Everything in our relationship would be blamed on how nasty, mischievous, dirty, and conniving women were. Men were never to be held accountable and men were rarely bad. My partner would talk cold hard trash about women but any given man was always a good guy, that is unless he looked twice my way.

I considered this mindset as a result of my partner's own traumatic experiences, and I wanted to offer myself as a relationship that proved different and helped to break down those barriers in the process.

Investing myself in my partner's healing became the biggest influence in my decision to stay in the broken relationship. Every problem that appeared was approached with a similar mindset - I would be the woman to show him different.

I will honestly say that all of what I experienced took place first because I did not take the time to be courted, to date, and to explore my partner *before* getting involved. I trusted him before he earned it and I committed myself to him before being aware of what and who I was committing myself to. If I knew what I know now, I would have changed how I engaged in dating this man. I would have taken my time, and I would have had boundaries for what I would and would not accept from a relationship.

Within a month or two, my new partner was my boyfriend and my king. He could have my body when he wanted it, he lived in my home, he received breakfast, lunch, and dinner and I spent all of my free time with him and him only. My life quickly changed from caring for myself to caring for myself and my new man. I didn't know at the time, but he would grow more and more needy and more and more demanding and what I thought I was giving freely, soon became a requirement.

I think this is the nature of a good woman - to be vulnerable, compassionate and a help-mate to someone we care for. Many of the broken love stories that I've heard from other women began with a similar mindset - they just wanted to be the woman to help change his mind and his ways and to show him how good of a lover they could be.

Ultimately, this is the strength of a woman. This is where we shine and have the ability to elevate our men. But when we offer this to someone who has no intentions or ability to reciprocate, it can dig us deep into a relationship that may not benefit us in the long run.

I don't think it's wrong for us to approach a new relationship in this manner but a change should occur when we experience an act of abuse. Abuse should not be something we work to fix. Abuse can only be something we identify and distance ourselves from. If your partner is going to fix their own internal problems, they will need time and space to do so.

Being a help-mate will always bring good favor back into your life, especially when it's given to the right source. My only advice to myself and other women working to identify the source of someone's behavior is to observe at all costs, draw barriers around what you will and will not accept within a relationship and act accordingly when barriers are crossed.

Abuse is a barrier that should never be crossed and if it is, that should be the queue to leave.

Protecting yourself starts at the beginning stages of a relationship. Your ability to do so effectively will determine the love you welcome into your life.

Nurture what is good and beneficial not only to your partner, but to you as well.

Chapter 9

THE TURNING POINT

Just when Michelle thought about leaving her relationship for good, things seemed to settle.

She'd been dating Dwayne for two and a half years now and through all of their ups and downs, Dwayne had stayed with Michelle and she had stayed with him. Their story wasn't the perfect love story but it was a survivor story and Michelle knew how to survive all too well from her own past circumstances.

It had been six months since they last had any type of physical altercation and they'd been going to church together as well as counseling here and there.

The couple was used to each other and had grown an

unbreakable bond. As far as the world was concerned, they were perfect. Both good looking, both successful, and both bound to have a wonderful future together.

What the world didn't know was that behind closed doors things weren't always as they seemed. Dwayne made it a point to stay active on Michelle's social networking. He encouraged her to post pictures of him often to keep her DM's quiet and so the world could see how good he 'treated Michelle'. He'd post a picture or two here and there as well, but it was a requirement for Michelle. If she didn't post every couple of weeks, she had to be cheating or hiding something as far as Dwayne was concerned.

So, she kept up with the posts and charades. She was happy that he wanted to show her off and be shown off. Most of Michelle's past relationships weren't open to pictures on social networking. Plus, it was a sign to Dwayne's exes that he was off the market and still with Michelle. That bit of comfort was satisfying enough given the infidelities they'd experienced in the past.

"At least Dwayne is trying," Michelle thought.

For the most part, the couple did everything together. It was only when it came to Dwayne's children and impromptu nights away that they were ever apart. For the most part, all of Dwayne's spare time went to Michelle. She was thankful that after all of the chasing she did during their early stages together, Dwayne was finally coming around to be the family man she had hoped for.

Yes, Michelle carried the bulk of the load, but that's what

strong black women do. While Dwayne was working to establish himself, she'd allowed him to move into her place. It helped with the cheating and gave Michelle the opportunity to show Dwayne how good of a wife she could be to him in the future. She was already used to handling her own, so it was nothing to continue that with her man there. The plus for her was knowing his whereabouts and getting that good loving whenever she wanted.

Well, whenever he'd allow for it.

Dwayne was still calling all of the shots.

He'd have her pussy when he wanted it and Michelle would always submit to his needs. As far as he was concerned, she was perfect for him. Michelle was well aware of this mind-set because of all the work she put in to go above and beyond what was expected. She didn't leave room for Dwayne to sneeze without a tissue and bless you following suit within seconds.

Michelle was on her job and Dwayne benefitted in every way possible from shelter, to meals, to security, to sex, to freedom and a home for his children if he needed it. Michelle was 'alla that and more'.

So why she continued to be disrespected was beyond her.

Michelle had grown used to Dwayne's ways but she desperately needed him to start carrying his weight around the house and to work on his attitude. All of the work Michelle was putting in was fine at the beginning, but it had taken a toll on her over the years and coming home to Dwayne's nit-picking and arguing was beginning to test her last nerve.

She was so deep into the relationship that it was hard at this point to know how to find relief. She kept reminding herself how strong she was, how it would all work out in the long run, and that self-motivation kept her pushing.

Michelle had lost contact with many of her friends. There was not enough time in the day to keep up with them anymore, but when an invitation from her best high school friend's wedding came in the mail, she had to make plans to attend.

"You have been invited to the King and Queen's wedding on June 17, 2019 please RSVP for you and your guest no later than May 2, 2019."

As soon as Dwayne came home Michelle was ready to share the news.

"Baby. We gotta take a trip to my hometown. My bestie's getting married!!" She smiled, danced to her own little jig and showed him the invitation.

"Best friend?! Woman, I'm your best friend! I ain't even ever heard you talk about this girl."

He handed the invitation back to Michelle with a frown.

"I told you about, Angie! Remember the girl I went to prom with because we both didn't have dates!? I tell you the story all the time!!" Michelle said playfully.

"So what, you going home for this or something?"

"WE! We're going home for this!"

Dwayne continued rummaging through the fridge for a drink.

"We're going! You'll get the chance to meet some of my friends from back in the day and I'll get the chance to catch up with everyone. It's going to be lit! Trust me, you'll love it!"

"Whatever you say, baby."

The couple ate dinner and Michelle began daydreaming about her upcoming trip home....

Michelle's best friend's wedding day had finally arrived and she could hear wedding bells in the distance and was dressed to the TEE!

Dwayne was equally sharp with a fresh cut, suit, and stylish striped tie that Michelle had picked out for him so that the couple could waltz the night away in style.

As they headed out of their home and into Michelle's Land Rover in style, Michelle just knew it was going to be a night to remember.

While Dwayne wasn't as excited as she was, Michelle spoke with him a week prior, urging him to be a good sport for the cause and gassing his head about how great the event would be. He took the time to listen and understand and the couple felt good about the event and even their planned attire.

Now they day was here and all that was left was for the couple to attend and enjoy.

The wedding was pure bliss. Michelle's best friend was from Sierra Leone and had a beautiful ceremony filled with African rituals, poetry, and song. Dwayne and Michelle listened intently and shared a moment of love in the ceremony that seemed to help them remember the end goal of their blossoming relationship.

Marriage, while beautiful, would take some time to prepare for, but the couple felt the magic and wanted to move forward with their love together, one day. They shared small talk about this in between the ceremony and reception and now it was just time to dance the night away and party!

The reception was equally beautiful. After the family had finished all of the photos, they entered the reception in the most luxurious tribal wear you had ever seen. Beautiful shades of blue, green, white, and gold filled the room and the faces of everyone in attendance were of awe.

Michelle was so happy for her best friend and was finally able to really catch up with both her bestie and a number of old friends that she'd spotted at the ceremony. It didn't take long for guests to start making their way over to Michelle with comments about "how long it's been" and "how beautiful" she looked.

Dwayne sat in the distance and seemed a bit irritated but took the time to introduce himself and shake hands with everyone that made their way over to Michelle. Michelle wasn't sure of the exact reason behind his irritation so she pulled him aside to make sure he was enjoying himself.

"Dwayne, baby, you cool?" She kissed him lightly on the cheek.

"Don't be kissing me now you wasn't kissing me when ol' boy was all up in your face"

"Dwayne, baby, don't be silly. Ain't nobody in here been all up in my face. If anything, these flirty girls been all up in…"

"Shut that shit up, Michelle!" Dwayne barked.

"Whoooaaaa whoooo whoooaaaaa," Michelle joked. "Calm down now partner."

She took the time to rub his hand and kiss him on the cheek once more.

"Baby," Michelle said, "I'm all yours. ALL yours. If any of these fellas even had a chance I'd have given it to them way back when. With you looking this good, trust me, all I'm thinking about is you."

"Okay..... Yea......you better....." he grumbled but calmed with Michelle's touch and compassion. "Aight, let's go back and wrap this up. I'm ready to get some real food and your people bougie as hell."

Michelle laughed.

"Okay, bet."

The two returned to the party hand in hand and made their way to the dance floor to shake a leg and loosen the moment. The evening was still on the up and up and since Michelle was well aware of Dwayne's temperament, she didn't pay his outburst too much mind. At least he's here, she thought to herself. Prior to the wedding she was sure he'd make a fuss to not attend. She was thankful her man was by her side and her family and friends could finally meet and interact with him.

Michelle was so lost in her own thoughts she didn't notice the man Dwayne was irritated with had been staring at her all night. She'd known the brother to have a crush on her in the past but it was never reciprocated so it wasn't a big deal to her at all. Dwayne, on the other hand was becoming livid.

As the couple said their goodbyes and Dwayne stepped away to get a slice of cake to-go, this brother made his way to Michelle for a final goodbye and hug. Michelle thought nothing of it and shared a few quick words before feeling a tap on her back.

"You got something to say to my lady?!" Dwayne interjected.

The mood of the whole interaction seemed to take a turn.

The brother from Michelle's childhood brushed it off and proceeded to introduce himself to Dwayne.

"Nah, I don't want to meet you." Dwayne replied coldly.

"Baby, don't -"

"Don't what, Michelle?! Let this man all in your face come at you right in front of mine?!"

"It's not like that," Michelle replied as the brother took this as his exit line to say that final goodbye and move on.

He reached to Michelle for a hug in the midst of saying goodbye and suddenly Michelle's feet flew from under her.

"Don't touch her!" Dwayne barked as he grabbed a handful of Michelle's hair and pulled her away. The strength and surprise of his grip sent Michelle tumbling to the ground and it seemed at that moment the entire wedding party came to a halt.

"Don't you ever touch my woman!" Dwayne stood toe to toe with the brother while Michelle laid on the ground in pure disbelief.

By this time several gentlemen in the wedding party had

helped her to her feet but Dwayne's eyes laid dark and stared directly at this brother who had just tried to hug his woman.

He suddenly turned abruptly, grabbed Michelle by the wrist and stormed out of the wedding party.

Michelle was distraught, fed up and humiliated.

As they made their way to the car she couldn't help but burst into tears.

"Shut up. You know what you was doing! Smiling back in his face while he smiled all up in yours. Bitches. Y'all a trip - I tell you that." Dwayne rambled on until all of his frustrations were voiced and then he fell silent and totally dismissive of Michelle's mere presence.

There was no accountability.

No apology.

No reasoning.

No discussion.

Nothing.

Silence as they drove home.

Silence as they laid down for bed.

Tears in Michelle's eyes.

A look of disgust in Dwayne's.

Michelle wondered how they'd ever get past this. And now, she realized just how exposed that moment made what others thought to be a 'dreamy union'.

Chapter 10

SUPPORTING
A LOVED ONE IN NEED

The phone calls had started and Michelle didn't really know how to respond.

She'd sheltered what she knew about Dwayne from everyone as best she could but his outbursts were getting more and more outrageous and more and more visible to the world around them.

The wedding was the first time Michelle's family and friends had been made aware of her life behind closed doors and they had questions about her safety.

Michelle knew that it was natural but she had no plan on

how to answer all of their questions.

"What's wrong with him?"

"Has he done this before?"

"Does he hit you?"

"Why does he talk to you like that?"

"Does he have jealousy issues?"

Michelle avoided call after call and text after text for weeks following their encounter at the wedding. She thought that with time they'd go away, but every time she picked up the phone to call her family, she knew they'd been made aware of the encounter (if not witnessed it themselves) and would continue with the questioning.

"Fuck it. I won't talk to any of them," Michelle thought.

The truth of the matter was that she needed them. She needed her family. She needed to know she was loved unconditionally and not as much of a fuck up as Dwayne constantly made her feel.

But now, she feared, in their eyes - she was a fuck up.

Silence was better than all of the questions.

The tears would dry with time and she would get through her battle with Dwayne in private, as every relationship should.

But this wasn't 'every' relationship.

Michelle was on a ledge with only she and Dwayne standing at the edge. She was sure if the rocks beneath them crumbled, Dwayne would save himself before he reached out to save her. This was the reality of their relationship and had begun to be the reality of other aspects of the couple's life.

Michelle was there to be a help-mate to Dwayne, but when she needed the same, she could only depend on herself.

The isolation and pain that Michelle felt weighed heavy on her and also began to bleed into other aspects of her life. Michelle had been late on her rent due to helping Dwayne with an unexpected expense. She'd been on her last leg at work due to all the calling in she'd been doing to manage things at home.

Michelle's health was suffering as well and she'd gained weight she never imagined gaining so quickly. The cute, fit and energetic Michelle was suddenly a shell of herself. Fifteen pounds heavier (and counting), acne prone, diet all off track and mind all over the place. Her once outgoing personality was now timid and shy. Her confidence was low and she couldn't even remember what she wanted out of life any more.

Michelle noticed that there was a change but she didn't notice just how visible it was beginning to become to others as well....

Supporting a loved one who may be a victim of abuse can be very complicated, but it is MOST necessary. This is not a responsibility you want to take lightly, but you also must realize that for a change to occur, it must be initiated by the victim. You cannot change their circumstances. You can only attempt to help them see the value in themselves and the destructive nature of their relationship.

Some general things to keep in mind as you consider your approach are that the abused are likely to have lived in a state of confusion for some time now. Help that looks like control will be difficult for them to accept. The damaged mind will be so exhausted from meeting the controlling nature of the abuser that anything that even looks similar could send them running. Your help must come from a place of compassion and genuine care. Remember that support for your loved one is sometimes as simple as a check in with no agenda!

Because of the emotionally draining nature of abuse, much of the victim's energy is likely to have been depleted by the abuser. Therefore, any reminder to the abused of their humanity, their value and their worth, will be welcomed. Remind them that they are loved. Remind them of how funny, sweet and accomplished they are! Make your conversations all about them and celebrate them as if there is no one on this earth that will celebrate them if you do not.

During conversations like this, don't even mention the abuser and if the abused brings them up, redirect the conversation back to them! It will be so important and valuable for the victim to still experience life outside of their relationship and it's important that they have conversations centered around themselves and not their abuser. There is value in true friendship and the shelter that it provides. Keep your loved one aware that they can always find a friend in you.

As we take a deeper look into support there are some aspects of it that I found very helpful as I began to break away from my abusive relationship. There are also aspects of support I wished for but did not get.

Support is:

- Compassion
- Love
- Direct
- Informative
- Non-Judgmental
- Patient
- Warm
- Consistent

First, support to a victim needs to come from a place of compassion and love.

Please understand that while you may have heard rumors or witnessed bits and pieces of abuse, you do not have a full picture of what your loved one has experienced; therefore you should tread lightly and offer yourself as a safe place for them to find relief. Abusers often carry other traits that encourage victims to isolate themselves or feel insecure about others. Offering yourself as a source of compassion and love can directly negate the feelings of isolation the victim may feel because of their circumstances. It's a powerful bit of love that could possibly help to break the cycle of abuse within the victim's life.

While you may have your own personal frustrations around why the victim has allowed themselves to be abused, check those feelings at the door or don't offer support if you cannot remove yourself from that mentality.

Abuse can be very overwhelming to the victim and the demands of their abuser could be taking up more of their life than you imagine. Having another party come in and offer demands for the victim to leave, or make considerable changes, could be very overwhelming. This sort of pressure could turn them away from you and even cause them to guard themselves from other forms of support in the future.

If you want to help your friend, start with compassion and don't let yourself be flustered if it's not met with welcoming arms. The compassion you provide in every encounter will plant seeds of comfort that the victim can come back to when they have the strength. Come from a place of love and the victim will always have an idea of where they can receive love from.

If you cannot come from a place of compassion and love, consistently, I encourage you to support with a more hands-off approach to avoid dumping any more toxicity into the victim's life.

Next, support to a victim is direct and informative.

I touched on the struggles of the black family earlier and we do need to consider that much of what we see is historical. I don't encourage you to approach the victim with facts, statistics, and spreadsheets, but if they've opened up to you and have been receptive to your compassion and listening ear, sprinkling in knowledge here and there could be a great bit of insight to help the victim look at the bigger picture of why the occurrence is happening within their own lives and the long term impact it could have.

While some of us may be well versed on our history, others may not feel comfortable with that approach. We are in the age of technology and being informative and direct can come in many different forms. From offering the victim resources on self-love techniques or developing barriers within relationships, to sending them links to meditation techniques or local retreats for women with similar circumstances, there are a ton of options available. I enjoy thinking outside the box when finding a solution to any problem. I encourage supportive loved ones to do some soul searching and educational digging of their own to help arm them with supportive resources that cater to the victim in question.

Again, we can't be pushy, demanding or belittling in our approach. If the victim isn't feeling the conversation, drop it. If they aren't feeling the resources, email it to them or drop it off in the mail instead and let them do with it what they may. It's your responsibility to plant seeds, but it is unreasonable to think that you can change their circumstances for them. That's why you're offering support and not a yellow brick road out of the circumstances they've chosen to be a part of. The choice to leave or repair their circumstances is the victims and the victims alone.

Another part of being direct and informative is being honest and upfront with the victim about what you've witnessed and why you'd like to offer support. Sometimes, victims can't see the big picture when they've been overwhelmed with all of the details or in the midst of chaos within their home. Sometimes just being made aware that their circumstances are visible outside of the home could help the victim understand just how damaging their situation may be. It takes true tact to know how to approach this with someone who's already hurting, but if you are a family member or friend with a deep connection that can have this sort of talk with your loved one, I encourage you to at least try. They may never hear it from anyone else if you do not.

Next, support is non-judgmental.

I can't stress this enough.

Being a victim of abuse is belittling and scary enough.

I personally got to my lowest point of insecurity in the midst of my abuse and that insecurity bled into my work life, friendships, and the outlook I had of myself. I was overwhelmed with the discomfort of never meeting my abuser's needs and always working so hard to only be told that it still wasn't good enough.

As a victim, you already feel a sense of shame for even seeing yourself in the circumstances of abuse. There are also a ton of feelings and emotions that come directly from the abuse that are overwhelming, belittling, and shameful. The last thing a victim wants or needs is another eye of judgement glaring in their direction.

Don't assume you know what the victim is going through. Even if you've experienced it, their story is their own and you have no true insight into the depth of it. Don't assume that it's easy for them to get out. You really don't truly know what's keeping them there. Don't assume that they are better than their circumstances. While that may be true to you, it must also be true to them and reach them on a deeper level to encourage their departure. While judgment is natural, it has no place in the support of your friend and should be checked at the door and not presented to the victim in any form or fashion.

Next, support is patient and it is warm.

You are your loved one's source of love. If you can't offer anything else, offering that is enough.

Are you aware of any type of abusers who are consistently patient or consistently warm? I certainly don't, which means this is a void in the victim's life that you may be able to fill. Please don't expect that they will change overnight or only come to you once with their concerns. No. You may hear the same type of story over and over and over, as long as you will listen.

Some think that's enabling. I consider it love.

If your loved one doesn't choose to leave, it could be difficult for you to witness, but imagine how difficult it is for them to bear. They need you. They need your listening ear. They need your love. If you can give it forever, please do so. They may never receive it from anywhere else and will need to remember, one day, what love truly is. Offer it.

Last, but not least, support is consistent.

Imagine offering the best level of support only to never offer it again. Imagine what that could feel like to the victim. It's not everyone's job to offer consistent support but if you are a close loved one or friend that could offer it, I encourage it. If you don't have the strength to offer support for the long run, don't hurt yourself trying, but offer some other type of support that can be provided at a distance.

Once I publicly shared my experience, I had a huge wave of support from family, friends, and acquaintances all offering check-in's, resources and well wishes to my moving past my circumstances. However, once all the dust settled, I was still alone and left to leave my relationship the best way I knew how. I went through my breakup for over a year and only had consistent support for about a month of that year.

Support under these types of circumstances needs to be consistent, even if it's just a quick check-in just to love on the victim. Honestly, often times those types of check-ins are the most valuable. People these days aren't pulling out the phone to take pictures when they're holding a face full of tears or considering hurting themselves to find relief. They're taking pictures and posting the good moments online.

We are in a time where our ideas of a person are based on social networking check-ins and not real-life phone calls and visits that offer back and forth communication. Because of this, a lot of people aren't checking in on their friends who seem to be doing just fine on the *internet*. Reminding the victim that they have a source of love and someone who cares for them could be even more relieving than talking about the abuse. Some victims don't want to talk about the abuse at all and you may have to connect with them in a different way.

My abuser constantly brainwashed me into thinking I

was in competition with other women, that my family and friends didn't truly care for me, that I had no value outside of him and that no one truly cared for me unconditionally - except for him. I was never that close to my family so it was easy after time for me to begin to internalize these thoughts.

With no family checking in, years went by where I grew to truly fall victim to my abuser's attacks. At first, I reassured myself that he was crazy and none of it was true. I thought of myself so strong minded that his tactics would never work.

I was listening to a TD Jakes sermon during a part of my journey that really opened my eyes to a new idea. The sermon spoke about the power of motivation and going to church to hear the word and then being uplifted by that motivation for the next week. TD Jakes then went on to speak about how negative communication can have the same effect. When you listen to negativity on a consistent basis, it has an influence on your walk and can negatively impact your thinking. Your thought process and mentality will begin to degrade itself over time and the negativity that you hear will begin to become your reality.

I experienced this and it is so very true. I want my abused audience to know that you are not stronger than his words. If you hear them enough, you will internalize them and you will see changes in your own mentality with time.

Supporters of the victim should keep this nugget of information in mind at all times so that it can influence your approach. Offering a victim another source of influence consistently could help them to remember their true value and that someone in this world still needs them in their lives.

Let that someone be you.

Chapter 11

MAKING A CHOICE FOR YOUR FUTURE

Michelle's Aunt Vicki called again for what seemed to be the hundredth time...

Ring...

    Ring.....

        Ring.......

"Hello", a shy and shaking voice responded from the other line.

"Michelle, baby?"

"Yes, Auntie?"

"Hello my Michelle, it's so good to hear from you. How

are you sweetheart?"

"Look, I'm sorry for not returning your calls but I really don't want to talk," Michelle responded.

"I understand! Baby I just missed hearing your voice and wanted to check in. How are you?"

"I'm good, Auntie..."

"Well, you're not sounding good! But if you say so, I'll have to just believe it. I've been calling your brothers and sisters and everyone says they can't get in touch with you. We're all worried, Michelle. I know you just think we want to get all in your business, but - "

"See!" Michelle yelled, "That's it! That's ALL ya'll want to do and I can tell you right now I'm FINE!"

"Michelle, look, I didn't call for all that but from the sounds of your tone, you're far from just fine. Now if you don't want to talk to your family about your business, that's just fine, I won't pry. But as for you and your well-being, I do need to know that you're okay before I hang up this phone."

Michelle's Aunt paused for what seemed like forever.

"Auntie, I think I need someone to talk to. I don't want to hear your opinion, but I really need a chance to just vent."

"That's what I'm here for 'Chele. Come on over anytime you want."

An hour and a half later, Michelle did just that.

"Auntie it's like I've been holding this in for so long and now I just need to know what I should do." Michelle looked to her Aunt for a response.

"Baby, matters of the heart take time... I can't tell you

what to do. But I can tell you that what you've expressed to me in the past hour seems to have taken a lot out of you. I want you to be alright with whatever decisions you choose but keep in mind, you have to have a healthy mind to go anywhere in life and it seems like you've kept a lot bottled in for quite some time now."

"I just wish I knew the answers. I wish I could read the future. Will he ever change? Is he the right man for me? What do we need to do to just get on the right page..." Michelle played with these ideas out loud until her Aunt bought her back to reality.

"Michelle, it's not about what the future holds. You'll never know what the future holds if you can't get through what's in front of you. Your life now needs to reflect what you want your future to be. That's how you use your power within to shape your own future. Take life for what it is. Uncover your own self-discipline and use it where you are weak. Draw boundaries for others around what you will and will not accept. When those boundaries are crossed, limit those relationships and bring balance back to your life."

"Please my Chelley...know that you are loved. And anything that's hurting you in life can be replaced with something that brings you joy. I love that beautiful smile of yours. To remove it in the name of "love" would be a sin! No one who loves you and knows how to love you properly will take away that pretty smile and on a consistent basis at that. No one."

And with that, Michelle's Aunt drew her in close and gave her a tight knit hug like she used to when Michelle was a little *girl. Her Aunt always had a way of helping her to release whatever pain was pent up inside of her and Michelle felt renewed from just getting her hurt off her chest and out into the universe, vocally.*

While she didn't know what she would encounter on the way back home, she felt comforted knowing that someone in life was still on her side. From there on out Michelle and her Aunt made a pact to meet up and get pedicures at least every other week and Michelle's Aunt made her promise to never get so isolated in her own world that she forgot about those who loved her unconditionally.

Ultimately, you only have two overarching choices in dealing with an abusive relationship. You, the victim, must choose to *stay* in the relationship or *leave* it all together. The choice is yours and yours only.

If you're like me, you'll go back and forth between the two options for several months or even years before actually making a choice, and it can be an even longer stint of time until you actually take action towards that decision.

Be patient with yourself.

You will need to be 100% comfortable with your decision for you to then act on it. This part of the relationship is the most difficult, in my opinion. Sure, it's not desirable, but all that you have to do to be a victim is sit there and deal with your abuser's stuff. Making a choice to leave takes action on your part.

Let's visit what each choice really means and the impact that it can have on the victim's life.

CHOOSE TO STAY

Staying in an abusive relationship doesn't always have to be a bad thing. More often than not, if we are choosing to stay it's because we can either endure the pain or we are confident that it will change. Either way, staying is keeping yourself in a vulnerable place and you will want to consider the impact that can have on your life.

If there is no hope for change, do you really think that you can endure several more years or even a lifetime of the same treatment?

Take some time to self-reflect and be honest with yourself about that question.

If you had to go through the year you've endured, for the next five years, would you be okay with that? Because only you will deal with it. Only you will mend your broken heart. Only you will tend to your wounded body and self-esteem. Only you will take care of yourself mentally and physically after an occurrence of abuse.

If you have children, not only will you have to take care of yourself, but you will still be responsible for their well-being and care after occurrences of abuse. You will also have the responsibility of explaining to them the instances of abuse that they may have witnessed.

Do not leave your children as confused as you are. They will be actively working to make sense of their environment and since you have sheltered them within it, you will be responsible for helping them to make sense and continue to grow, despite it. Remember, you chose to endure the abuse, but they did not. Make sure you have put your children's well-being in the forefront of your mind and that your decision benefits their growth. You will have little control over the actions of your abuser, but all the responsibility when it comes to mending and repairing yourself and/or your household. If you do have children or are with child, I urge you to consider staying in your abusive relationship as a *last* resort.

For some time, I considered staying with my abuser and helping him to work towards a more fruitful relationship with me as my choice. For the last year of our relationship, I tested this approach. We put resources in place to help us get to a healthier place - counseling, church, discussions with more established couples, more time apart, more transparency and truth, etc. These were all tactics that we tried in one way or another to get past the abuse and offer resources to help us when tension ran high. Some tactics worked for a little while, but none helped to mend the true cause of the abuse.

When it came down to it, my partner had to want to for himself and not for the sake of the relationship. The behavioral changes that he needed would take time and true dedication. While marital counseling and group sessions were helpful, they could never totally dissipate the abuse without my abuser taking responsibility for his part in initiating the mental and physical abuse.

Every time I decided that I would work to mend the relationship and not leave, I endured another few months of abuse. It didn't look that way at first. We'd almost always have a month or two of peace before the next occurrence. But, the next occurrence would always happen and almost always be worse than the last.

The more I chose to stay, the more I would be belittled and the more outrageous the belittlement would get. Sometimes, when he knew I was fed up to my limit, he would stop one form of manipulation and abuse and opt for another. I noticed that as I learned him, he learned me as well! My abuser could work me right up to my limit and then pull back and sprinkle in a sweet or kind gesture to take the attention away from his belittling treatment. If I still chose to end the relationship, he would blame the break-up on me, as if I were unreasonable and just looking for a reason to abandon him in his time of need. This tactic would always make me feel guilty and bring me right back into the arms of abuse.

I'm still at a loss for whether or not my abuser was a pure genius, or if it was in fact just *that* easy to manipulate me. This sort of thinking is exactly why abuse and manipulation can be so daunting. Instead of looking at your abuser, you look to yourself for the answers to make it all stop. This mentality plays in our abuser's favor. If you're always looking at yourself and trying to change yourself, you don't have the capacity to see them for who they really are and the hamster wheel they have you running in.

So, ladies, if you stay, just understand that situations like this typically get worse before they get better. Be ready for a rocky road because only time will truly change a person, and since you will be a part of their change, you will also suffer (or be relieved by) the circumstances and outcome.

Please keep in mind that these are individuals whose life circumstances or lack of emotional growth has led them to this place. There are even some abusers who enjoy the nature of the abusive relationships they ensue. I remember my ex acknowledging to me once that he had to have someone he could be mean to in his life. Behavioral changes take a desire to change and then active support and resources to initiate the change.

It is unreasonable for you to think that your abuser will change in a short time. However, if leaving the relationship is out of the question for you, the one caveat to consider when deciding to stay is whether or not you can remove access to yourself physically as your abuser initiates change. In my honest opinion, this is the only form of choosing to stay that should be considered.

Again, this is something that I tried myself. It failed for me. It failed because instead of the time apart being looked at as an opportunity for my abuser to mend himself and find his own self growth, he instead took the time to brainstorm and consider ways to manipulate me from afar. My abuser also became paranoid at the idea that I might be entertaining other men and often times just that thought alone could cause him to lash out at me, my property or mental space.

Staying, even at a distance, proved more hurtful to my relationship and individual well-being than making the choice to leave. Ultimately, even if you choose to stay but create distance, you will have to leave the relationship in order for this approach to offer the healing that your partner needs to evolve.

No one can judge those who choose to stay. Even though onlookers will, you have to make the best decision for you. Abuse looks different for everyone and maybe there are some abusers who can be changed. Only you know your circumstances and personal limitations, and you have to decide based off of that. My only suggestion is to be smart, aware of reality and to always choose you and your physical and mental well-being, first.

CHOOSE TO LEAVE

Choosing to leave your abusive relationship is a decision that takes true courage. If you're on the path to leaving your relationship, feel comforted in the fact that you are taking the road less travelled and making a decision that will have a huge impact on your future and the future of your relationships.

First, take a moment to just celebrate yourself on this major decision.

I'm not going to lie to you and say it will be easy. Leaving my relationship proved to be one of the hardest things I've done in my adult life. If you're new to the abuse and not too tied to it, this may be an easier process for you. If you've been in your relationship for some time or are tied to it through marriage or children, this may be a little more difficult for you.

Be patient with yourself through this process. Know that there are no right answers and the process of leaving can be quick or it can drag out. Take the time to understand and digest your previous experiences in the relationship so that those memories and experiences can help you to prepare yourself for road-blocks along the way.

For example, if you know that your abuser is combative and revengeful, you should prepare yourself to experience aspects of that while trying to leave. Anything that you can do to mentally and physically prepare yourself for this transition should be taken into consideration before making the move or even discussing your plans to leave.

Because abusive relationships don't just happen overnight but through a process, I encourage you to take care of yourself - leaving the relationship may not happen overnight either.

I shared with you that first, I tried to stay. I worked to mend the relationship as a unit instead of apart. After that approach failed, I made several decisions and attempts to leave. I went through another six months just trying to put physical distance between myself and the mate I was trying to leave. My abuser did not let go without a fight. On each occasion that I tried to leave, I experienced one, if not several, forms of backlash that included more physical abuse and mental abuse geared towards making me feel guilty and shameful. I dealt with attacks against my character, to my family, his family and friends, threats to make sexual content shared within the relationship public to outsiders, attacks on my property and belongings --- just overall chaos!

If I thought that things were bad within the relationship, the fight that my partner put up to keep me was even worse. I'd go through ebbs and flows of him trying to attack or scare me to death and then work his charm on me to win me back. This was one of the most confusing and unsettling times of my life! I couldn't understand why when I was with him, I seemed like a total fuck up and no matter how much I did to prove my love, I could never please him!

On the other hand, my leaving seemed detrimental to him and like the worst possible thing I could ever do! If the idea of my leaving was SO bad, why couldn't my mate just meet me where I was within the relationship so that we could both be happy? I pondered this question in my mind for so long and honestly, still do! But this is the nature of abuse and dealing with someone whose ability to foster a healthy relationship is just not there. It's going to be confusing, it's going to be conflicting, and it's just not going to ever really make sense until they get the help that they need to change their relationship approach.

I don't doubt that my partner wanted to be a good mate. I don't doubt that the love was there. But, the ability to find healthy outlets for his energy, the ability to respect me and even respect himself, and the ability to foster a love that could benefit us both was not there. My partner's insecurities, his rage, his inability to compromise and add value to my life controlled his approach to the relationship and overshadowed any bit of peace that we both worked to bring to the table.

This is why it's so important to take the time to understand your circumstances, evaluate and reevaluate them, and then make a plan that makes sense and one that you can stick to. If you make a choice to leave but continue to go back, life is going to be very difficult for you. If you choose not to make a choice and stay in a state of confusion, your mental and emotional health will be impacted and you'll be living in a state of confusion instead of a state of peace.

Leaving will bring you peace. Leaving will bring you peace because no one can operate at full capacity if they do not have stability within their home. You are setting yourself up for failure.

Think back to your childhood years and the classmates that you knew of who had difficult circumstances at home. Teachers review students' personal circumstances and keep a list of "at risk" students to help them prepare for the levels of support they may need to offer that year. Teachers do this because they understand the consequences of having an imbalance within a child's home.

Children who are not nurtured and given a safe place to grow at home suffer the consequences within other aspects of their lives and often times need additional support.

It's the same for adults!

If you continue to stay in a dysfunctional relationship that's never stable and often times in a state of stress - your life is going to be impacted. Your friendships are going to be impacted. Your work is going to be impacted. Your outlook on life and so much more is going to be impacted until you bring peace and stability into your life.

Yes, you can choose to stay. By all means, do what's best for you! But if you are interested in legacy building, laying a foundation for your family, growing and accomplishing your own personal goals and involving yourself in the community, you are going to find that very difficult to do with a part of you attached to your goals and another part of you attached to abuse.

Choose to break the generational curses that our parents could not. Choose to foster a healthy relationship and household and allow those suffering from abusive personalities the time to mend and heal themselves in the process.

Michelle had a choice to make.

Should she keep dealing with Dwayne's drama or make the choice to leave?

On one hand - she loved him dearly and felt he needed a positive influence like Michelle in his life.

On the other hand - she was drained from offering the levels of support he needed while still being treated with no regard to follow.

Michelle felt that while she was perfect for Dwayne, she was empty for herself.

She knew she wasn't healthy mentally or physically.

Two months after the wedding incident, Michelle made the choice to leave Dwayne in order to make a better life for herself.

"There is nothing more I can do here," she told herself as she prepared to break up with Dwayne that night.

Michelle ran errands, read motivational quotes, and listened to motivational speaking all day just to mentally prepare herself. She wasn't sure how Dwayne would take the news. He hadn't been physical since the wedding, but he had been distant ever since. Michelle wondered if she'd ruined their relationship by attending that wedding. A part of her knew she should be able to live the life she enjoyed while still having a romantic partner, but that was just not the case with Dwayne. It was his rules and his rules only and anything outside of that could get ugly.

So, Michelle let Dwayne get settled in and about an hour after arriving home, she pulled him into the living room to talk.

"Dwayne, I'm not feeling valued in this relationship. I've been feeling this way for some time now and nothing I do

seems to make it better. I think it's time for us to take some time apart to work on ourselves and reflect on whether or not this is the right relationship."

Dwayne started laughing, "Girl please, you ain't goin' nowhere." He sat back, amused.

Michelle spoke carefully.

"No. I'm not going anywhere. But I'm asking you to leave within the next thirty days. This relationship is just not working for me."

"Not working for YOU?! And you got me out here looking like a fool in these streets and you want to tell me this relationship ain't working for you?!"

"Yes, Dwayne."

"Well okay you little princess bitch! I'll pack my bags and be out next week."

And with that Dwayne breezed past Michelle and on into the bedroom where he turned on the television, kicked back and enjoyed the rest of his evening silently.

Michelle thought to continue the conversation but at the end of the day, she was getting what she ultimately knew was best. There was no purpose in arguing, she'd just let Dwayne be a jerk until the thirty-day mark was up.

Chapter 12

DEALING WITH
THE AFTERMATH

Twenty-four days later Michelle was worse than
she'd ever been.

After Dwayne realized the truth behind Michelle's decision to leave the relationship, his disrespect and treatment of
Michelle worsened and his disgust for her was apparent.

A week earlier, Michelle found a woman's clothing
that was not her own present in their bedroom. When she
addressed it with Dwayne, he denied it with an aloofness that
sent Michelle up the roof.

"This is MY home! I pay the bills here. How dare you

have another woman in MY home!"

"You kicked me out, remember?! Ima do what I want til next week then I'll be out your hair for good. My new chick moving me in and you think you on but she shits on you. You could never be her."

Dwayne's words cut deep and it seemed every day he aimed to belittle Michelle or make her feel insecure in one way or another. Enough was enough.

"Get out!!" Michelle yelled.

"Shut that shit up. You ain't gonna do nothing but call your old ass auntie or the police anyway."

"Get out!!!!" She yelled and bucked at Dwayne. Michelle didn't know what had gotten into her but she couldn't take another day of this!

As she lunged towards Dwayne he took his bottle of water and through it on her and spit in her face.

"Yea, what you 'gon do? Don't play with me Michelle. Calm that shit down before you get hurt."

Michelle grabbed the closest object she could find, a knife on the kitchen counter and threw it at Dwayne hitting him in the arm. Luckily, it was the handle end of the knife but you couldn't tell Dwayne that Michelle hadn't stabbed him - he took the knife, grabbed Michelle by the neck and held the knife to her neck.

"Oh, you 'gon try to kill me, huh?! You wanna see me dead, huh?!" Michelle tried to get away and Dwayne spun her around and slammed her to the ground, pinning her there. She struggled with all her might but his weight dominated *and exhausted her. Within seconds, she gave up.*

"Yeaaaaaaaa. Yea you little bitch remember who daddy is. Remember who your boss is. I do what I want. I ain't going nowhere. Tell whoever you want! They ain't 'gon save you." He shook her by the shoulders, one time, with force and got up.

As he brushed his shoulders off and pulled himself together, Michelle lost control, picked up the knife and stabbed Dwayne in the back.

He fell to the ground, blood began to flow from his wound and Michelle passed out....

Moments later, Michelle woke up to Dwayne calling the police.

"Yea this bitch stabbed me! Come now - come now and arrest this bitch! I need an ambulance, fuck somebody come NOW!!!"

Michelle wasn't sure if she should pretend to still be passed out or run. She opted for the latter and jetted towards the door.

"No, bitch! You not going nowhere! You'll pay for this!"

Dwayne had a fire in his eyes that Michelle had never seen before. She thought he'd pick up the knife and kill her right there. Instead, he blocked the door to keep her from leaving and opened it once the police knocked.

"Hello sir, can you tell me what happened here."

"Yea this bitch stabbed me! You see it! She stabbed me!!! Arrest her, arrest her right now!!!"

The officer took the time to take both Dwayne and Michelle's statements.

They both walked away in handcuffs.

The relationship ended by force and now all Michelle had was the painful memories, a lost job due to the arrests and jail time to follow, and a hazy outlook of herself and her blazing failures.

Michelle's life had been ruined.

She made the choice to leave too little, too late and the effects changed the trajectory of her life...

To those that choose to leave their abusive relationships - again, I applaud you.

I cherish and appreciate your efforts, and I want you to recognize just how much power you've placed in your own hands regarding your future.

You're taking the first step towards freeing yourself from bondage and making a healthier choice for you and your legacy. You will be restored and you will be blessed with a good and fruitful love in the future.

But the story doesn't stop here.

I'm not going to lie and tell you that just making the choice and distancing yourself from your abuser will be the end of your battle, because it won't.

As I sit here in tears writing the story of my failed and abusive love story, the only life I've known for the past several years.....I write in a manner that you might feel my pain so that you can bear with your own. While our stories may differ, I find the pain and frustration around this occurrence so strong that where we might differ, the pain that we feel inside is universal. It's okay to hurt, it's okay to not be okay all the time.

This is a difficult journey and one that seems to never have an end when you're in the midst of it. People may have a ton of feedback and suggestions but the journey will only be experienced by you.

I made the choice to leave. My abuser did not.

The tug and pull of these dynamics left me in a lonely, black hole of a place that I thought I could never recover from.

The dynamics of the love battle. The dynamics of outsiders' opinions and judgements. The isolation of not being able to share the true depth of your experiences and pain. The pain of looking at the broken you and then trying to come up with a plan for recovery.

It's very overwhelming and you may experience consequences of the aftermath well after actually physically removing yourself from the situation.

In regards to the love battle - I tried for a very long time to have this all make sense to my abuser so that I could feel freed within my decision.

There is no such understanding that you can gain from someone who chooses to manipulate, control and belittle you. In their unhealthy state, I do not think people under this umbrella truly have the compassion necessary to understand and truly sympathize with the pain they have caused.

I got lost in trying to prove my worth, my faithfulness, my efforts and even the validity of my choice to leave to my abuser. In doing so, I gave him even more control of my mind and I depleted much of my own energy source for a goal that would never come to fruition. Never once did my abuser sympathize with my pain, never once did he take the time to truly understand it. All that ever came from these efforts were more reasons that I should live in guilt and shame.

This is the nature of abusive relationships and the abuser and victim dynamics. If you're on a similar path, I beg you to stop. Your decision to leave requires no disclaimer, no announcement, and no convincing of anyone but yourself. Save your energy for the battle that's ahead of you.

The world and your abuser will never give you the okay to choose you and your happiness. When you make that choice, understand that it will be a very personal choice that only you can give yourself affirmation for. If you're able to get it from family and friends, by all means use that energy to help restore yourself, but if you have to do it all alone, that's okay too. There are others out here, just like you struggling to find their way but nevertheless on the path to it.

You are strong beyond what others can even imagine and you will have to take time out to remind yourself of that.

I'm going to be honest - I'm still dealing with a conditioned mind. My abuser still has as much power over me now than when we were together. I write this book in the midst of my decision to leave, and I sit here in tears writing this chapter and reflecting on the Nicole that I am today.

The Nicole that I am today is broken. I suffer from depression, especially at night. I suffer from insecurity, bad thoughts of myself, a mistrust of men and people in general, and so much more.

There is a part of me that wonders if I will ever get back to the old, healthy me. The easiest way for me to ignore my depression would be for me to open myself back up to my abuser. Feeling his closeness and knowing that he accepts me, even though his acceptance hurts, can still bring me comfort.

I'm aware now, however, that this comfort is a false sense of peace and it is only a temporary relief. I have to be honest and aware of my thoughts during this stage of my life. Only through acknowledging my thoughts can I be honest about my state of growth and progress in healing. I have realized that my healing will take time and there is no microwave fix for this sort of thing. I fight with the idea of going back to my abuser daily. It's hard because he still actively pursues me and offers me a home in his painful arms of love.

When I experience the urge to go back to my abuser, I have to also decide on whether or not I want to band-aid my pain, or heal it. Going back to my abuser, while he is still in an unhealthy state of mind, will not offer me healing and I have to continue to make a decision to not band-aid the pain, but to remove it.

I think this internal battle is the hardest that's come but there are still other challenges within this process that I'd like to share.

When you speak out about your abuse, if even just to your family or friends, you open yourself up to others opinions, ridicule and judgement. If you are strong enough to accept that, use your story to teach others, but if you are not, I encourage you to move in silence until you are free.

When a person uncovers that they have been abused, it is at the expense of their abuser. There is no way around it. Any time a person speaks out about someone who's hurt them, it's going to expose the person they've spoken out about. This is why it's so easy to take sides, make up stories, and pass judgement. No one wants to look at someone they love in a negative light. A person's romantic partner is bound to know them on a deeper level than the rest of the world.

My abuser was charming and established in his community. I was new to HIS area so the difficulties of our relationship weren't accepted by those in his circle. Because I was so caught up in him for the duration of our relationship, his circle was my circle and it seemed to me that everyone around me was looking at me with disgust. I never experienced this sort of ridicule and my depression worsened under the weight of it.

The insecurities I felt in my relationship then deepened as I learned just how alone I really was. People that were once considered family and friends took this time to openly share their disappointment and the compassion that I desired was few and far between. I found myself paranoid at work and within new relationships. I saw no value within myself. Internally, I was lost with no life line in sight.

Reality and the insecurities within my own mind began to blend. I went through many months of just fighting battles within myself and working to restore the confidence I once had. No one will understand until it's them going through it. Yet everyone will have an opinion to share with you.

People are going to ask - 'How does he still have access to you', 'Why is he still a part of your life', 'Why are you entertaining him'. With those questions there is an underlying notion that you must be doing something to egg it on.

Outsiders are not always aware of the nature of abusive relationships. How captivating and addicting they can grow to be, even for the victim. They aren't always aware of the levels that abusers will go to continue to keep their victims in mental or physical bondage, even years after the relationship has ended.

As you receive feedback, suggestions and even opinions, take them with a grain of salt. Keep what's valuable and discard the rest. Your emotional well-being will depend on your ability to do so.

To leave your abuser is to have a continuous internal battle, a battle with your abuser, and a battle with outsiders' perceptions of your reality. Only time and consistency will bring each of these battles to an end. If you go back to your abuser during this process, you will put yourself at risk of a relapse and you will have to start the process all over again.

Leaving an abusive relationship should be like kicking an alcoholic addiction. You may need to wean yourself off to break free, but once you do break free, you have to resist from going back at all costs, or the wound will burst back open and deepen with each occurrence.

This is a process that you're going to want to give up. There will be times that you do give up, and a weak moment may send you spiraling back to your abuser and into a state of confusion all over again.

If that happens, it's okay, be honest with yourself, hold yourself accountable and start the process all over again. You made the right decision for yourself, and in weakness and in health, you will have to continue to make that right decision and bring yourself out of this current state of abuse that you're in.

Continue the healing process until it becomes all that you know and the abuse is just a memory.

It's going to be hard and it's going to hurt like hell. You are leaving someone you loved and you are also limiting the feeding of your own internal addiction to the abuse. Your body and mind want to be fed by this painful pleasure but you must fight the urge to return and replace it with the urge to heal.

Push through the hard times, forgive yourself for your mistakes, and truly offer yourself compassion and peace during this time of your life.

You deserve it.

Choose you.

Chapter 13

HAPPILY EVER AFTER IS A MINDSET

A year later, Michelle walked into the doors of Shang Town High School with confidence and an aurora that she'd never had before. She walked on stage, in front of a group of forty plus students, and told her story.

She spoke with such clarity and conviction that the entire room stood in applause at the end of her speech. Ladies kept her there for two more hours just to ask questions and gain inspiration from her experience.

Michelle was empowered and fulfilled - for once in her life, she knew she was taking charge and moving forward with her true life purpose, which was to be an example for others, and to use her pain to rebuild her local community.

It had taken a long time for Michelle to get to this place. After not only losing Dwayne, but also her freedom and almost, her mind - she was finally recovering and moving on to bigger and better things.

Michelle wasn't happy with her past, but she had learned from it. After the incident with Dwayne, Michelle was charged with Aggravated Assault. She could not afford a lawyer and had to settle for a public defender, who was able to get her a plea deal that only required her to be incarcerated for four months with two years of probation. While the instance still left a salty taste in her mouth, she thought - better that than to be dead or out of my mind.

Honestly, Michelle was thankful for her time away. She got to see Dwayne for his true self after he called the police on her, knowing the pain he had put her in. But it was good that she took the time away. It forced her to cleanse herself from the relationship and begin reflecting on her own life and value.

Michelle spent all of her time locked up reading and studying about abuse, self-love, healthy relationships, and positive black role models. This awareness helped her to build her confidence back up and it helped her to establish guidelines for healthy living in her own life. She made a goal that if she made it through this intact, she would give back to the community and share her story with whomever needed to hear it.

A few months out of jail, Michelle was doing just that......

Sometimes you have to lose it all to actually find you. Michelle was happy with the woman she'd become and she would never again let a man take away that power.

Yes, her story held her pain, but in evolving, she was able to release it.

Michelle was finally whole.

Chapter 14

TO MY ABUSER

To the men and women who abuse others....

You are powerful without question. I encourage you to understand the purpose of your power and how to best utilize it.

When you bring mental and or physical abuse to another, you are demoralizing their very existence. You are taking a person that the Universe blessed you to love, and instead putting them in a hurtful state of confusion that they may never have the opportunity to recover from. You are taking a person who could be an angel in disguise, or have great purpose over their life, and you are stripping them of their value as a human being.

If that is your hope, God bless you and your soul. Your soul will never find peace or true comfort through your actions and you will live in a state of hate for the majority of your days. You will never know what true love feels like because the people in your life will operate in a state of fear and resentment. They will not be able to step outside of the pain they are enduring and into a place of love. Even if they choose to stay with you physically, you will be missing out on the true depths of their love emotionally.

You will never receive true love from those you victimize.

If your hope is for a change within your own life. I encourage and applaud your understanding that healing is necessary. I encourage you to take steps towards that healing because wishing for it just isn't enough.

If you are on a path of recovery, you are as necessary to our communities' growth as those working to remove themselves and heal from abusive relationships. Your healing will take time, action, and supportive resources. I encourage you to seek the healing that in turn is seeking you.

We need you to be whole before you choose to love again and I urge you to remove yourself from dating and romantic relationships until you have found the peace, healing and growth within yourself so that you can turn you away from your abusive ways.

I pray for even you. I find true value in those who choose to run from the demons within themselves in order to replace them with something more fulfilling and fruitful.

In saving someone from the broken you, you are turning a victim into a survivor and I applaud you for that powerful step.

I wish you all the best in your journey towards that growth.

CPSIA information can be obtained
at www.ICGtesting.com
Printed in the USA
BVHW070027171021
618930BV00001B/61